P9-EES-086

Published by

 **THE GENERAL STORE PUBLISHING HOUSE INC.**

General Delivery, Burnstown, Ontario Canada, K0J 1G0
(613) 432-5990

ISBN 0-919431 02-X

Printed by Donald F. Runge Ltd., Pembroke
Photos by Allan de la Plante

Canadian Cataloguing in Publication Data

Bennett, Jo-Anne, 1952 -

The Complete Gas Barbecue Cookbook

Includes index.
ISBN 0-919431-02-X

1. Barbecue cookery. I. Title.

TX840.B3B45 641.7'6 C82-090143-1

THE COMPLETE gas barbecue cookbook

by Jo-Anne Bennett

Open Letter

As with all new products and ideas, there is a period of testing that goes on during the initial stages. The employees of B.D. Wait Co. Limited, the Canadian manufacturer for **Wait Broilmaster** gas barbecues, are indeed privileged to have had their barbecue used for the testing of the recipes contained in this book.

We at B.D. Wait have enjoyed several of the delicious meals presented to us by Jo-Anne and her kitchen crew.

May we extend hearty congratulations to Jo-Anne for a job well done and to you the barbecuer, who we are sure will enjoy **"The Complete Gas Barbecue Cookbook"** as much as we do.

All of us at B.D. Wait

Introduction

As far back as I can remember, the arrival of nice weather meant one thing, Barbecue Season. I often wondered why my parents had a stove in their summer cottage on the Ottawa River, for it was never used. Of course, rain was an occasional hazard, but my father eliminated the problem by building an open porch, primarily to enclose the barbecue.

My first experience in barbecuing by myself was when I was eight years old. After a day spent catching bullfrogs in a nearby swamp, by brother and I cleaned and skinned them and roasted the legs over an open bonfire. Frogs' Legs in a fine restaurant have never tasted as wonderful.

Over the years, I am certain, we have tried every type of barbecue and barbecue equipment but nothing has compared with the innovative gas barbecue. No longer do we have to wait until the "coals are ready" or worry about running out of them. How often have you had late-arriving guests show up just in time to see the last of the charcoal turn to ashes?

Proper timing is an integral part of any good cook's expertise and a gas barbecue makes it all possible. Upon converting from charcoal to gas, we found there was quite a difference in cooking time and methods. Gas cooks much more quickly. And so, to save you the tragedy of overcooked food, we present **The Complete Gas Barbecue Cookbook** with our best wishes for a successful Barbecue Season.

"To the memory of my best friend and partner-in-crime, my brother, Paul Matthie."

Jo-Anne Bennett

Contents

Obtaining Good Cooking Results With Your Gas Grill

Cooking outdoors on a gas grill should be a delightful experience. You can cook a great variety of foods to please your family and friends. However, your cooking skill with your barbecue will increase as you become acquainted with the grill and how it operates.

Charcoal Flavor Without Charcoal

Charcoal has no flavor. It is odorless and flavorless. The so-called "charcoal flavor" is imparted to the meat by the flare-up and smoke resulting from the dripping of meat juices and fat on the hot charcoal. The same kind of flare-up and smoking results from the meat juices that drop onto the hot Flower Rock coals of your gas grill. You can prove it to yourself.

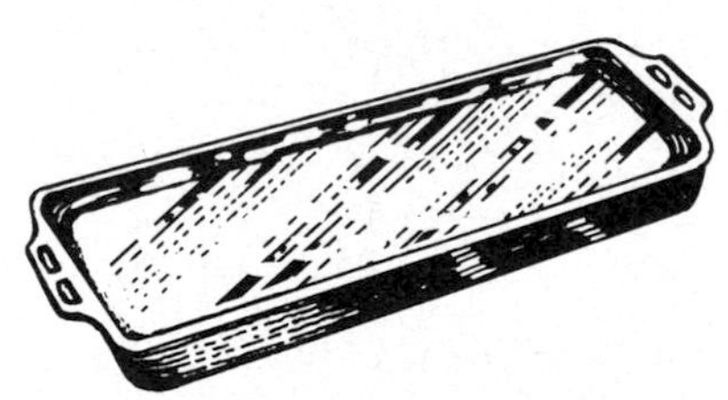

Charcoal Grill Versus Gas Grill

Here are the differences:

Before you begin to cook, it is important that you understand how gas differs from charcoal cooking. Charcoal is consumed in use. Once ignited it slowly burns up, reaching a peak of heat output, then gradually burning away to ash. Therefore, it is necessary to add additional charcoal if cooking temperatures are to be maintained over a period of time.

Instead of combustible charcoal, your gas grill uses non-combustible volcanic rock known as ''Flower Rock''. The ''Flower Rock'' coals--chunks of volcanic rock that never burn up--are distributed over a rack and are heated in the gas flames.

It is easy to maintain constant cooking temperatures in a gas grill because the gas burner is infinitely adjustable.

Basic Operating Instructions

Preheating the Grill

Before each use, preheat the grill with the cover closed and valve knob on ''Hi'' until the Heat indicator reads at least 400 degrees. **REMEMBER**—the grill broils better when the Flower Rock ''coals'' are hot because the grease dripping on them flares up and imparts that great barbecue flavor to the meat.

Adjusting the Lid Position

Most gas grills can be operated with the cover completely closed or completely open, or at several different levels of partial opening. This variation enables you to further regulate and maintain cooking temperatures by controlling the flow of air through the grill. With some foods you may also prefer leaving the lid open slightly to allow excessive smoke to escape.

Ways to Cook With Your Gas Grill

Surface Broiling With Lid Lowered (or closed completely)

There's no question--you get more flavor when you broil or cook with the lid of your gas grill lowered or closed completely. Therefore, this is by far the most popular method of cooking among barbecue users.

Meats and foods cook more quickly when the cover is lowered, because heat is confined in the grill and both the top and bottom surfaces of the meat or food are exposed to cooking temperatures.

You get more flaming and more smoke, and therefore, more smoky flavor when the lid is lowered or closed--but be careful, or you will over-char and over-cook the food. When broiling hamburgers or steaks, most users will use the Hi burner setting--particularly if they like their meat rare or medium. This method insures quick searing and charring of the outside surface without overcooking the centre of the meat.

Your own experience will quickly acquaint you with this method of cooking, so you will know what burner settings will produce the cooking results you want, and whether to close the cover or prop it open a bit.

Surface Broiling With the Lid Raised

This method of broiling exposes only the bottom side of the meat or food to cooking temperatures. It is the slowest method of cooking on a gas grill, and is therefore, suitable only for foods that cook quickly.

People who don't particularly care for smoky flavor may prefer this method because it provides the least "barbecue" taste. For obvious reasons, it is not a good method when the weather is cold or windy.

Roasting, Baking or Barbecueing

By closing the cover of your gas grill you can also make it an oven. By means of burner adjustments and the Heat indicator, you can control the temperature inside the grill and use it to bake, roast, or barbecue a great variety of foods.

For example, you can bake potatoes and vegetables in the closed grill, and then keep the potatoes hot on the potato rack while broiling the steaks, hamburgers or whatever!

Rotisserie Broiling

The most popular accessory for gas grills is the electric or battery operated rotisserie. The flat rotisserie broiling basket is an equally desirable item. Together they make rotisserie broiling a great method of cooking on your gas barbecue.

Rotisserie broiling offers these advantages:

1. **Meats brown and cook evenly on all exposed surfaces.**
2. **Rotisserie-broiled foods do not require constant attention.**
3. **Whole turkeys, whole hams, large roasts can be cooked or barbecued with delicious results.**
4. **Exact degree of done-ness can be easily determined by the use of meat thermometer.**

(Note: Not all meat thermometers are meant for use on a gas grill. Do not leave in meat.)

Foods that cook best on a rotisserie, using the regular meat clamps, are whole turkeys (if pre-basted turkeys are used you must be careful of extra flaring) and hams, rolled roasts, rump roasts, sirloin tip roasts, loin roasts, large fowl, leg-of-lamb and any other bulky cuts of meat that can be properly impaled and balanced on the spit.

Foods that cook best on a rotisserie, using the flat basket, are chicken halves and quarters, beef and pork ribs and fish.

Whether to Rotisserie Broil With the Grill Lid Raised or Lowered?

Meats cooked on the rotisserie with a lower burner setting and the grill lid partially open will usually be more tender and have a more smoky flavor. Use of the lid stop to adjust opening and maintaining desired temperatures is important in rotisserie cooking. Most people prefer to have the valve in the "Lo" position and the lid stop adjusted to provide a 2 ½" opening. This method of cooking exposes the meat to a combination of broiling and baking. It is an outstanding and flavorful way to cook meat or fowl.

Closed Cover Broiling or Baking

Many outdoor cooking enthusiasts use this method most of the time. They like the smoke and flames and the extra smoky flavor it produces.

Many backyard chefs grill steaks (preferably thick), chops and hamburgers with the burner on "Hi" setting and grill cover completely closed. This method produces quicker cooking, more browning or charring of the meat. It is particularly effective in preparing rare steaks or chops, because it quickly sears and browns the outside of the meat while leaving the inside still appetizingly rare.

For slower cooking the burner should be at a lower setting. A combination of a lower burner setting and partially raised lid will produce cooking temperatures in the 275-350 degree level which is needed for slow cooking or broiling. Slow cooking insures maximum tenderness and less shrinkage of all kinds of meats and fowl.

Used as an oven, your gas grill achieves marvelous baking results. It's great for roasting foil-wrapped corn on the cob, vegetables of all sorts, potatoes.

Or use it in place of your kitchen oven (especially on hot days) to cook a pan roast, bake a ham or prepare any "main course" that would heat up your kitchen and make your air conditioner work harder!

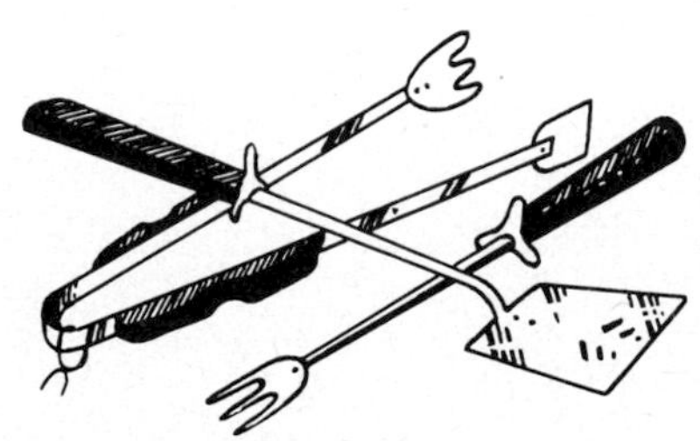

Use of Twin Burner

For those times when the entire cooking surface is not needed to prepare your meats the twin burner affords an excellent way to conserve gas. You can light only one of the burners (either left or right), cook your food on that side of the grill and, if needed, use the other (unlighted) side to keep already prepared foods warm.

When, however, there is occasion to prepare a larger or more varied menu, the two, individually controlled burners are an excellent advantage. For example, you can use one side of the grill to rotisserie broil a roast or chicken with the burner on that side set at the appropriate temperature. At the same time, with one or two of the grids in place, you can be cooking a casserole dish, potatoes, or other vegetables, to complete the meal. Or if you are using the entire cooking surface, one side of the grill can be set at a temperature suitable for those wanting their meat rare (usually high flame, with the grid or grids positioned closer to the coals). At the same time, the temperature control on the other side of the grill can be set for more well-done meats. Your own experience and needs will teach you the variety of ways the twin burners can be used.

Indirect Cooking

It's a great way to bake, roast or barbecue beef, pork or fowl, especially a turkey. You simply operate one burner and place the meat or fowl over the other. Cooking heat radiated and converted from the operating burner surrounds and cooks the meat or fowl on the other side of the grill.

The indirect method of cooking is especially effective when you want to cook slowly without the meat or fowl coming in contact with flames.

Flaming and Smoking

A reasonable amount of flaming and smoking is desired in broiling or cooking most kinds of meat because it produces the "barbecue flavor" that is the essence of outdoor cooking.

Too much flaming, however, can cause burning and charring of the meat and should be avoided.

To reduce or eliminate flaming:

a. Trim surplus fat off meat or fowl before broiling.
b. Use ground chuck or round for hamburgers. Ordinary ground beef is usually too high in fat content for good broiling results.
c. If a pre-basted turkey is to be cooked, keep a close watch for excessive flare-ups; these turkeys are filled with oil.
d. Cook with the grids at top level, and, if necessary, burner at lower setting.
e. Flaming may be controlled, in some cases by adjusting lid stop to hold the lid open slightly.

Broiling and Cooking Times

A cooking time chart is not an exact guide for operating a gas grill, because you will be cooking outdoors where temperatures and wind can influence rate of cooking. Different barbecues, size of the meat and how often the lid is raised also have an effect on cooking times.

There is no better way to insure good cooking results than close attention to the meat or food on the grill. If you are cooking thick cuts of meat or whole fowl use of a meat thermometer is your best insurance of exact cooking results. But be careful. Some meat thermometers, left in while cooking, can give false readings. Your best guide is your own experience in the use of your gas grill. You will soon become expert in gauging the amount of time needed to cook various foods and meats to the desired degree of done-ness.

If your gas barbecue does not have more than one cooking level, simply adjust your temperature control. For example, if the recipe calls for using the lower grill over low heat, then the middle grill over medium heat is comparable. So that you may compare the distance from the flame, on the barbecue we use, it goes as follows:

Lower grill - 3 inches from flame
Middle grill - 4 1/2 inches from flame

Remember, when in doubt, it is safer to increase the heat gradually and avoid the risk of burning a well-prepared meal.

Preventive Maintenance and Safety

For Your Safety

IF YOU SMELL GAS

1. Shut off gas to appliance.
2. Extinguish any open flame.
3. Open grill lid.
4. If odor continues, immediately call your gas supplier.

Do not store or use gasoline or other flammable vapors and liquids in the vicinity of this or any other appliance.

Keep electrical supply cord and gas supply hose away from any heated surface.

Location and Minimum Clearances

If your gas grill is to be located close to the house or any other combustible surface, observe these minimum clearances:

Edge of broiler to side wall: 16 inches (41 cm)
Edge of broiler to rear wall: 16 inches (41 cm)

The foregoing clearances will be obtained if 30 inches (76 cm) clearance is maintained from the centre line of the post to the side and rear combustible walls.

Keep the area around and under the grill free from anything that might obstruct the flow of combustion and ventilation air.

Do not install grill under overhead unprotected combustible surfaces!

Testing for Gas Leaks

Once all connections have been made, and valve knob (knobs) is in the "OFF" position, turn gas on at the source and check for leaks. Make a soapy solution with dish detergent and water. "Paint" every joint in the new pipe line and every joint in the old line that was tampered with. Bubbles, a hissing sound or an obnoxious odor indicate gas leaks. Turn gas off and re-tighten any connection that appeared to be leaking then re-test for leaks. Tighten and check all connections each time the cylinder is filled.

CAUTION: Never test for gas leaks with a lighted match! A small gas leak can produce a large flame.

NOTE: Always turn off the gas supply to the grill at the cylinder first. Then turn off the control valves, this will empty the gas lines and prevent rotting.

When the grill is to be stored indoors, the connection between the cylinder and the grill must be disconnected and the cylinder removed from the grill and stored outdoors in a well ventilated area. If the cylinder is not disconnected from the grill, the grill and cylinder must be stored outdoors in a well ventilated area.

To insure safety and good performance, I suggest all adjustments, servicing and replacement parts (such as burners, valves, and regulators) should be handled by your local dealer, your local gas company or a qualified serviceman.

appetizers

By way of introduction, may I present to you some of my favorite appetizer recipes, especially adapted to the gas barbecue. Whet your guests' appetites with these before-dinner treats and you can relax and enjoy the company without worrying if anyone is starving while awaiting the main course.

Rumaki

Bacon and Water Chestnut Roll-Ups

½ cup soya sauce
1 tablespoon sugar
1 - 10 ounce can water chestnuts
Sliced raw bacon

- Mix together in a small deep bowl, the soya sauce and sugar. Stir together to dissolve the sugar. Drain the water chestnuts, add to the mixture and toss gently to coat. Marinate for a couple of hours, stirring frequently. Drain and roll each water chestnut in a slice of bacon. Fasten together by skewering with a toothpick.
- Preheat barbecue on high and turn to low 2 or 3 minutes prior to adding Roll-Ups. Place on lower grill on a sheet of perforated foil for 7 to 10 minutes, turning frequently.
- Broil until bacon is cooked and serve hot. You may also cook Rumaki on a griddle for 12 minutes.

Serves 4 to 6

Clam Stuffed Mushrooms

1 pound fresh mushrooms
¼ cup butter
1 - 5 ounce can minced clams
1 garlic clove, minced
¼ cup dried bread crumbs
2 tablespoons chopped fresh parsley
½ teaspoon salt
Dash of pepper

- Remove the stems from the mushrooms and chop the stems up finely. Place the mushroom caps on griddle, hollow-side up.
- In a medium skillet over medium heat, melt butter. Brush some on the mushroom caps. Drain the liquid from the clams and add it to the butter, still on medium heat. Add the chopped mushroom stems and garlic and cook until stems are tender, stirring occasionally.
- Stir in the clams and remaining ingredients and remove from heat. Spoon the clam mixture into mushroom caps. Place griddle on middle grill in barbecue over medium-low heat. Cook for approximately 12 minutes until mushrooms are tender.

Serves 4 to 6

Cheese Stuffed Mushroom Caps

1 - 6 oz. package cream cheese at room temperature
1 tablespoon minced chives
1 tablespoon chopped walnuts
1 tablespoon chopped pimento
1 pound fresh mushroom caps

- In food processor, blend the cream cheese until smooth. Mix in the chives, walnuts and pimento.
- Remove the stems from the mushroom caps. Wash the caps and drain well. Spoon the cheese mixture into the caps and place, cheese-side up, on the griddle.
- Cook on middle grill over medium heat for 10 minutes, until the cheese is melted.

Smoked Fish Spread

1 pound smoked fish (See page 90)
1 cup mayonnaise
2 teaspoons minced onion
1 tablespoon chopped parsley
1 garlic clove, minced
1 teaspoon dry mustard
Dash of Worcestershire sauce

- Skin and bone the fish and flake into a small bowl. Add the remaining ingredients, mixing well. Chill. Serve with crackers.

Cheese 'N Onion Squares

5 slices light rye bread
½ cup mayonnaise
2 small onions, thinly sliced
10 stuffed Manzanilla olives
¼ cup grated Cheddar or Mozzarella cheese

- Cut each slice of bread into 4 squares. Spread squares generously with mayonnaise and place an onion slice on top of each one. Place half a stuffed olive on each onion. Sprinkle with grated cheese.
- Place on a griddle on the middle rack over medium heat for 12 minutes, until cheese is melted.

Serves 4 to 6

Stuffed Lobster Tails

½ cup soya sauce
1 tablespoon sugar
1 - 10 ounce can water chestnuts
2 - 8 ounce lobster tails
Approximately 10 strips bacon

- Mix together the soya sauce and sugar in a small, deep bowl. Stir to dissolve sugar and add the drained water chestnuts. Toss gently to cover. Marinate for a couple of hours, stirring frequently. Drain.
- Wash the lobster tails and remove shell by cutting the underside, lengthwise, with scissors. Pound tail flat until it is ¼ - ½ inch thick. Cut lengthwise into strips 1 - 1 ½ inches wide. Wrap each water chestnut with a strip of lobster tail and then a strip of bacon. Secure bacon and lobster tail with toothpick. Each lobster tail will make 4 or 5 roll-ups.
- Barbecue on middle grill over medium heat on a sheet of perforated foil for 15 minutes or until bacon is crisp and lobster is puffy white.

Serves 4 to 6

Bacon and Chicken Liver Kabobs

1 pound chicken livers
½ pound bacon slices

Marinade:
¼ cup soya sauce
¼ cup vegetable oil
¼ cup sherry
1 tablespoon Worcestershire sauce
2 tablespoons corn syrup
2 tablespoons brown sugar
2 teaspoons dry mustard

- In a deep bowl, mix the marinade. Cut each chicken liver in half, removing any membrane. Add the chicken livers to the bowl and marinate for one hour.
- Remove the meat from the marinade and wrap each liver piece in a bacon slice, securing with toothpicks. Thread these onto short (6 inch) wooden skewers (about 4 per skewer).
- Place on the middle grill, on top of a sheet of aluminium foil with holes punched in it over medium heat for 10 minutes or until the liver is tender and the bacon is crisp. Turn frequently. (The tinfoil is to prevent flare-up from the bacon drippings.)

Serves 4 to 6

Oysters-On-The-Rocks

Fresh Oysters (4 or 5 per person)
Lemon Pepper (may substitute lemon juice and black pepper)
Bacon Strips

- Shuck the oysters and drain off the juice, saving half of the shells. Sprinkle the oysters with lemon pepper and wrap each in a short strip of bacon, securing with wooden toothpicks.
- Place the oysters in the washed half-shell and place on the middle grill over medium-low heat for 15 minutes, until the bacon is crisp. Serve with lemon wedges and Seafood Sauce. (See below)

Oyster Kabobs

- Prepare the oysters the same as you would for Oysters-On-The-Rocks, discarding the shells. Thread the wrapped oysters onto 6 inch wooden skewers, leaving a space in between each, using approximately 4 per skewer.
- Lay the kebobs on a sheet of foil with holes punched in the bottom to prevent flare-up from the bacon drippings. Place on the middle grill over medium-low heat for 15 minutes, until the bacon is crisp. Serve with lemon wedges and Seafood Sauce. (see below)

Seafood Sauce:

½ cup catsup
2 teaspoons horseradish
Mix together well

poultry

Chicken

Chicken ranks high among North America's favorite foods. It can be fried, baked, stewed or broiled. It can be seasoned in limitless ways. Yet, what way of cooking makes this domestic fowl more delicious than broiling over an open fire?

Chickens for surface broiling should be fryers or broilers cut in halves and quarters. Cut up chicken dries out too quickly.

Surface broiled chicken

1. Preheat grill at medium burner setting for 10 minutes with cooking rack removed.
2. Locate cooking grid at top position. Rub surface of grid with cooking oil to minimize sticking.
3. Place chicken on grid, cavity side down. The cover may be raised or partially lowered. The chicken will cook faster with the cover lowered.
4. Turn chicken frequently and baste with melted butter, or a favorite basting sauce. If chicken is browning too fast, turn burner knob to lower setting.

Rotisserie-broiled chicken

Rotisserie-broiled is a favorite way of barbecuing chicken because it cooks the chicken to an appetizing, even brownness and requires less attention. Chicken may be cooked this way with the grill cover lowered to increase the smoky flavor. Whole chickens may be skewered and clamped and tied into position on the rotisserie spit. The spit will hold two average or three small broiler type chickens.

Halves and quarters of chicken can be rotisserie broiled in the flat rotisserie basket.

This basket will hold from five to seven chicken halves.

Chicken should be brushed occasionally with your favorite basting sauce to keep it moist and tender.

Chicken Wings

5 - 8 pounds chicken wings
Salt
Pepper
Garlic salt
3 tablespoons paprika
Vegetable oil
1 cup soya sauce
½ cup water
2 teaspoon sugar
3 - 4 tablespoons rye

- Lay the chicken wings out in one layer in a large pan and season with salt, pepper, garlic salt and the 3 tablespoons paprika. Let stand one or two hours or overnight in the refrigerator. Fry in oil until browned on all sides and drain on paper towel.
- Marinate for 2 hours or overnight in mixture made up of the soya sauce, water, sugar and rye. Stir occasionally.
- Remove the wings from the marinade and reserve the marinade. Lay the wings on a griddle or double-thickness of aluminium foil. Place on the middle grill over medium heat for 5 minutes, turning and brushing with the reserved marinade.
- Leave the lid up. These may be served cold as well as warm.

Chicken Burgers

2 whole large chicken breasts, skinned and boned
1 small onion, minced
1 egg
1 tablespoon sherry
1 tablespoon chopped parsley
¾ teaspoon salt
¼ teaspoon pepper
¼ cup mayonnaise
1 tablespoon vegetable oil
1 cup dried bread crumbs

- Cut the chicken meat into one-inch cubes or pieces and coarsely grind in a food processor or meat grinder. In a large bowl, combine the ground chicken, onion, egg, sherry, parsley, salt, pepper, mayonnaise, oil and bread crumbs.
- With hands, shape the mixture into 3 inch round patties. Flatten well as they will contract and mound up. Place on the lower grill over high heat for 8 minutes. Turn and continue cooking for another 8 minutes.
- Place on buttered, toasted buns and garnish with lettuce, tomato slices and mayonnaise.

Serves 4

Hungarian Chicken Breasts

Allow ¾ pound per person

3 pounds chicken breasts
½ lemon
Salt and pepper
Paprika

Baste:
½ cup melted butter
1 garlic clove, minced
½ teaspoon crushed thyme

- Place the chicken breasts in a shallow pan. Squeeze lemon juice over the top side of the chicken and sprinkle with salt, pepper and generously with paprika. Let sit for 30 minutes.
- Meanwhile, in a small bowl, mix the melted butter, garlic and thyme.
- Place breasts on the middle grill over medium-low heat for 40 minutes, turning and basting frequently until golden.

Serves 4

Lemon Chicken

1 3½ - 4 pound chicken, cut up
3 lemons
½ cup olive oil
3 garlic cloves, minced
1 tablespoon dried rosemary
1 teaspoon salt
¼ teaspoon pepper

- Grate 1 tablespoon of peel from the lemons. Squeeze out ⅓ cup lemon juice into a small bowl. Add the lemon peel, olive oil, garlic, rosemary, salt and pepper. Mix well.
- Lay the chicken pieces in a shallow pan and pour the marinade over it. Marinate for 2 hours in refrigerator, turning occasionally.
- Drain the meat, reserving the marinade. Place chicken pieces in grill basket with the spit rod through the centre. Place on the rotisserie over medium-low heat for 45 minutes to one hour, brushing with reserved marinade occasionally.

Serves 4

Drunk Chicken

- Mix equal parts of melted butter and beer in a bowl. For example, 2 tablespoons butter and 2 tablespoons beer. Baste the chicken frequently as you are barbecuing. It gives a lovely, golden crust. Excellent on ribs as well.

Barbecued Chicken

1 3 ½ - 4 pound roasting chicken
1 teaspoon salt
Pepper
1 - 2 tablespoons vegetable oil
½ cup catsup
¼ cup cider vinegar
¼ cup lemon juice
1 small onion, finely chopped
1 tablespoon brown sugar
1 tablespoon Worcestershire sauce
½ teaspoon chili powder

- Wash the chicken under cold water and pat dry with paper towels. Sprinkle salt and pepper inside the body cavity and close up both ends with small metal skewers. Tie wings up over the breast and tie legs together tightly. Insert spit rod through centre of cavity of chicken and secure with holding forks, at left side of spit. Place on the rotisserie over medium-low indirect heat for one hour. Brush the chicken with the vegetable oil.
- Meanwhile, mix together in a small saucepan, the remaining ingredients. Bring to a boil and simmer for 15 minutes, uncovered. Brush this mixture on the chicken and cook for an additional 30 to 45 minutes, or until legs move easily. The chicken should be brushed several times with the sauce until it is richly glazed. Leftover sauce may be served with the chicken.

Serves 4

Garlic Chicken

1 3 ½ - 4 pound roasting chicken
1 teaspoon salt
Pepper
½ teaspoon crushed oregano
6 garlic cloves, peeled

- Rinse chicken under cold water and pat dry with paper towel. Sprinkle salt, pepper and oregano in the cavity of the chicken and stuff with the garlic cloves.
- Close the cavities, securing with small skewers. Tie the wings together over the breast and tie the legs together, crossed over the tail, with heavy string.
- Insert spit rod through the cavity and secure with holding forks.
- Place on rotisserie over medium-low indirect heat for 1 ½ hours, until leg moves easily, brushing with Garlic Baste.

Serves 4

Garlic Baste:

2 tablespoons lemon juice
2 tablespoons vegetable oil
½ teaspoon garlic powder

Mix together well.

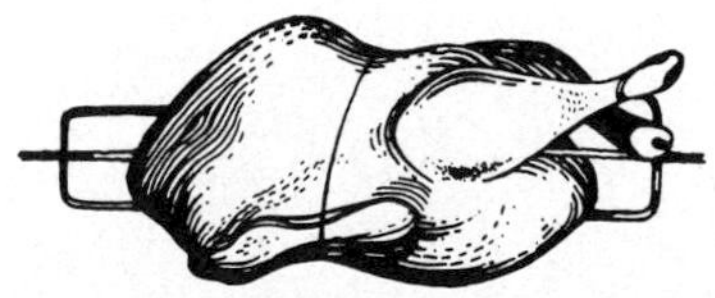

Stuffed Rock Cornish Hens

2 Rock Cornish Hens (about 1½ pounds each)
¼ cup olive oil
½ cup chopped walnuts
1 cup soft bread crumbs
1 small onion, finely chopped
1 cup chopped celery
½ teaspoon salt
¼ teaspoon pepper
¼ teaspoon crushed rosemary
½ teaspoon dried tarragon leaves

- Rinse hens under cold running water and pat dry with paper towels. Mix together the oil. walnuts, bread crumbs, onion, celery, salt, pepper, rosemary and tarragon.
- Stuff half the mixture inside each bird. Close the openings with small skewers. Tie the legs together and the wings over the breast with heavy string. Insert the spit rod through the centre of each bird and secure with holding forks.
- Place on rotisserie over medium-low indirect heat for approximately 1 ½ hours. Baste frequently with either Wine Baste or Orange Baste.
- Game hens are done when meat pulls away from the bones.

Serves 4

Wine Baste:

¼ cup melted butter
¼ cup dry white wine
2 tablespoons lemon juice
½ teaspoon dried tarragon leaves

Combine and mix well.

Orange Baste:

¼ cup frozen orange juice concentrate, thawed
¼ cup vegetable oil
2 tablespoons honey
½ tablespoon grated orange peel

Combine and mix well.

Cornish Hens with Pineapple

2 Rock Cornish Hens (about 1½ pounds each)
Salt and Pepper
2 tablespoons butter
Lemon juice
4 pineapple rings
4 teaspoons brown sugar
4 Maraschino cherries

- Cut the hens in half with kitchen shears. Sprinkle the cut side with salt and pepper.
- Place on the middle grill, cavity-side down, over medium-low heat for 10 minutes. Turn and place one tablespoon of butter in each cavity and sprinkle with lemon juice. Cook for 10 minutes.
- Place a pineapple ring on each cavity. 1 teaspoon brown sugar in each pineapple hole and a cherry on top. Cook for an additional 5 minutes.

Serves 4

Herbed Turkey Parts

3 pounds turkey parts, thighs and drumsticks
½ cup melted butter
¼ cup dry white wine
¼ cup lemon juice
½ teaspoon salt
1 garlic clove, minced
½ teaspoon chervil or tarragon

- Place meat in a shallow pan. Prepare marinade and pour over the meat. Marinate for 2 hours. Remove the meat, reserving the marinade.
- Place on the middle grill over medium-low heat for 40 minutes, turning and basting frequently until golden brown.

Hint: When basting, be sure to watch over the meat closely as flare-ups can occur. I find that moving the meat around a little will prevent it from burning.

Serves 4

Stuffed Turkey

Allow ½ pound of turkey per person

1 - 8 to 10 pound turkey

Stuffing:
1 pound sausage meat
4 cups crustless, white bread crumbs
1 ½ cups chopped pecans
1 medium onion, chopped
¼ cup chopped parsley
½ cup chopped celery
1 teaspoon summer savory, crushed
1 teaspoon salt
½ teaspoon pepper
1 tablespoon dry mustard
1 cup riced, mashed potatoes

- Rinse the bird with cold running water and pat dry with paper towel. Set aside.

- To prepare the stuffing, brown the sausage meat, breaking it up finely. Remove from heat to cool. Combine the remaining ingredients in a large bowl with the sausage meat.

- Fill the cavity of the bird only three-quarters full as the dressing will expand. Close both openings with small skewers. Fold wings close to the body and tie or skewer. Tie the legs together tightly. Insert the spit rod through the centre of the cavity, balancing carefully, and secure with holding forks.

- Place on the rotisserie, with a drip pan underneath, over low indirect heat, allowing approximately 20 minutes cooking time per pound. Baste occasionally with the pan drippings or some vegetable oil. Turkey is done when the drumstick moves easily and comes away from the turkey or the meat thermometer registers 190 ° F. Let rest 10 minutes before carving.

Smoked Turkey

1 6 - 8 pound turkey
2 cups hickory or apple chips

- Soak the chips in water for at least one hour. This will make them smoulder and create smoke and not burn.
- Rinse the turkey and dry well. Fold the wings close to the body and tie or skewer. Close both openings with skewers. Tie the legs together tightly.
- Insert the spit rod through the centre of the cavity, balancing carefully. Secure with holding forks. Place on the rotisserie over low indirect heat with a drip pan underneath.
- Throw half of the drained wood chips on the hot coals, adding more as they are needed. Be sure to keep the lid down and the smoke in. Baste occasionally with the pan drippings or vegetable oil.
- Cooking time will be approximately 2 ½ hours or until the meat thermometer registers 190 ° F or drumstick moves easily.
- Be sure to let rest for 10 minutes before carving.
- May be served hot or cold.

beef

Hamburgers

For flavorful hamburgers use a good grade of ground beef, ground sirloin, round or chuck. Avoid low-priced ground meat with high fat and gristle content. Besides lacking flavor, cheap ground beef "melts away" in the process of cooking.

Hamburger patties for broiling should be ½" to ¾" thick. Use a "HI" or MEDIUM burner setting. For a smokier flavor lower grill hood while cooking.

Turn hamburgers only once. Like cheeseburgers? Put a slice of cheddar cheese on each patty after it has been turned.

Hamburger patties at the outer edges of the cooling grill will need a little more cooking time. If you wish to accumulate cooked hamburger patties, use the potato rack. This will hold the hamburger patties far enough away from the flames to prevent over-cooking, but will keep them at serving temperature.

Choosing Good Steak for Broiling

For best broiling results choose sirloin, T-bone, Porterhouse, Filet Mignon (tenderloin), Club, Ribeye, and the related cuts, sometimes identified as "New York", "Kansas City", etc. The preferred grades are Prime and Choice.

For good broiling a steak should be from 1 ½ to 2 inches thick. One-inch thickness is minimum.

A thick steak can be broiled to an appetizing brownness on both sides without becoming too done on the inside, and it slices and serves better. A thin steak quickly becomes over done and dried out, and loses much of its taste appeal.

Tips for grilling steaks

1. Remove steaks from refrigerator one to two hours before cooking.
2. Trim off excess fat and suet, leaving a thin edge of fat. Score the fat to prevent curling during cooking.
3. Rub fat or salad oil on cooking rack to minimize sticking.
4. Do not salt meat while cooking; salt draws out juices and toughens the meat.
5. Turn steaks with tongs or spatula. Piercing meat with a fork releases juices and increases flare-up.

6. Use higher burner setting for rare steak, and lower burner settings for medium and well done-ness.
7. To increase smoky flavor, lower cover to one of three positions provided by the cover stop located on the left side of the grill, or close cover completely.
8. Generally the best, most flavorful method is achieved by broiling steaks with the burner on HI setting and the grill cover closed.
9. Do not leave steaks unattended. For the most delicious and appetizing steaks, be johnny-on-the-spot to turn and remove them from the grill just at the right time!
10. Like that Hickory taste? Sprinkle dampened hickory chips or sawdust on the briquets a few minutes before steaks are done and lower cover. The result--that hickory smoke flavor!

Ruthie Burgers

2 pounds ground beef
¼ cup chopped onion
1 egg
2 teaspoons Worcestershire sauce
1½ teaspoons crumbled summer savory
1 teaspoon hickory smoked salt
1 teaspoon pepper
1 cup dried bread crumbs.

- Mix all ingredients together. Shape into round, flat patties.
- Place on the lower grill over high heat for 10 minutes. Turn and cook for an additional 10 minutes. Serve on buttered toasted buns.
- Heat the buns on the upper rack while cooking the second side or toast on the grill.

Serves 6 to 8

Pineapple Burgers

- Prepare Ruthie Burgers or Gourmet Burgers. After cooking one side and turning, place a pineapple ring on each burger with a maraschino cherry in each pineapple hole.
This gives a whole different flavor to the burgers and is very attractive to serve.

Gourmet Burgers

1 pound ground beef
1 small onion, chopped
½ teaspoon salt
¼ teaspoon pepper
½ teaspoon garlic powder
2 eggs
1 tablespoon butter
¼ cup pine nuts
½ cup chopped fresh mushrooms
Dried bread crumbs

- In a medium bowl, mix together the beef, onion, salt, pepper, garlic and eggs.
- In a small skillet, melt the butter and add the pine nuts and mushrooms, frying until pine nuts are golden brown. Add to the beef mixture. Add bread crumbs until the desired consistency to make burgers is reached.
- Shape into patties with your hands.
- Place on the lower grill over high heat for 10 minutes on each side.

Serves 4

Honey and Garlic Ribs

4 meaty short ribs of beef
½ cup pineapple juice
¼ cup soya sauce
½ cup honey
1 teaspoon dry ginger
2 garlic cloves, crushed

- Place the ribs in a large pot and cover with water. You may add a teaspoon of salt and a sliced onion to this. Boil the ribs for 45 minutes. Drain well. Place in a shallow pan.
- Prepare the marinade by mixing together the remaining ingredients. Pour over the ribs and marinate for 2 or 3 hours, turning a couple of times. Drain, reserving the marinade.
- Place the ribs on the middle grill over low heat for 20 minutes, turning and basting frequently with the reserved marinade.

Serves 4

Beef Teriyaki

1 - 2 pound beef round steak, 1" thick
½ cup soya sauce
¼ cup brown sugar
1 garlic clove, minced
1 teaspoon dry ginger
1 tablespoon vegetable oil
1 small pineapple, cut into 1" chunks

- Cut the steak into strips, ¼'' wide and 2 or 3'' long. In a medium bowl, mix together the soya sauce, brown sugar, garlic, ginger, and oil. Add the meat and toss to coat well. Marinate in refrigerator for 2 hours, tossing occasionally. Drain, reserving marinade.
- Thread the beef on 18'' metal skewers, accordion-style, alternately with the pineapple chunks.
- Skewer the meat loosely and do so just before cooking as the pineapple tenderizes the meat very quickly and will turn it mushy.
- Place on the middle grill over medium heat, turning and basting with the reserved marinade for 20 minutes.

Serves 6

Beef Kabobs

1 ½ pounds beef top round steak or sirloin, 1" thick
½ cup red wine
¼ cup olive oil
¼ cup soya sauce
1 medium onion, sliced, in rings
2 garlic cloves, minced
2 teaspoons salt
1 teaspoon grated ginger
or ¼ teaspoon ground ginger
1 pound mushroom caps

- Remove any excess fat from the steak and cut into large cubes, approximately 1 ½ inch. Mix together the remaining ingredients in a large bowl. Stir in the beef cubes and marinate for 2 hours at room temperature or 3 hours in the refrigerator, stirring occasionally.

- Drain the meat, reserving the marinade. Thread the meat onto 18 inch long metal skewers, placing a mushroom cap between each piece of meat.

- Place on the lower grill over medium heat, turning and basting with the reserved marinade frequently, for 15 minutes with the lid down.

Serves 4

Steak and Nectarine Kabobs

1 pound round steak
¼ cup honey
¼ cup red wine
¼ cup soya sauce
1 tablespoon vegetable oil
1 teaspoon rosemary leaves
¼ teaspoon salt
1 small onion, in ¼ inch slices
2 nectarines

- In a deep, medium-sized bowl, mix together the honey, wine, soya sauce, oil, rosemary leaves, salt and onion slices.
- Cut the round steak into half-inch thick slices Add the meat to the marinade and toss to coat well. Cover and refrigerate for 2 hours, stirring occasionally. Cut each nectarine into four wedges.
- Remove the steak slices reserving the marinade. Thread the meat, accordian-style, onto 4 long metal skewers alternating with nectarine wedges. Use 2 wedges per skewer.
- Place on the lower grill over medium-high heat for approximately 12 minutes, turning and basting with the reserved marinade frequently.

Serves 4

Mushroom Meat Loaf

2 pounds ground beef
1 small onion, finely chopped
2 eggs
1 cup dried bread crumbs
2 teaspoons salt
½ teaspoon pepper
1 teaspoon crushed thyme
½ cup sour cream
1 cup catsup
1 cup fresh mushrooms, chopped

- In a large bowl, combine all ingredients. Place in an 8 inch loaf pan (aluminium) or shape into an 8 inch loaf and wrap in a double-thickness of aluminium foil. Secure well to seal in juices.
- Place on the middle grill over medium heat for approximately one hour. If using a foil packet, turn carefully every 10 or 15 minutes.

Serves 6

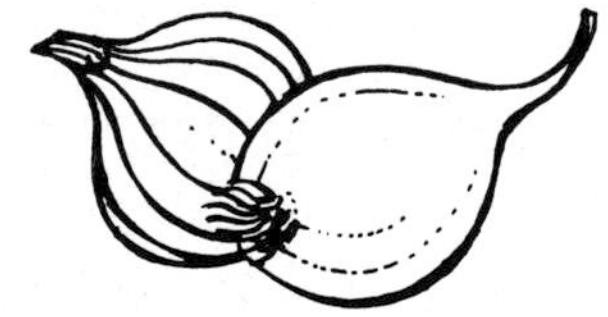

Sesame Sirloin

½ cup vegetable oil
¼ cup sesame seeds
½ cup soya sauce
¼ cup lemon juice
2 teaspoons sugar
¼ teaspoon pepper
2 garlic cloves, crushed
2 medium onions, sliced, in rings
2 - 2 ½ pounds beef top sirloin steak, 2" thick

- Mix together, in a small skillet, the oil and sesame seeds. Cook over medium heat, stirring constantly, until the sesame seeds are toasted. Remove from heat and mix together with the soya sauce, lemon juice, sugar, pepper, garlic and onions.
- Pour into a shallow pan and add the meat, turning to coat completely. Cover and refrigerate for 3 or 4 hours, turning steak occasionally.
- Remove steak from the pan, reserving the marinade. Place on the middle grill over medium heat for 15 minutes, basting occasionally with the reserved marinade. Turn the steak and cook for an additional 15 minutes, again basting occasionally.
- This cooking method will provide you with rare steak in the centre, medium on the outside. For well-done steak, increase your cooking time.
- To serve, place the steak on a large platter and cut into strips. Your guests may then choose according to their preference.

Serves 4

Sirloin au Poivre

2 pounds Sirloin Steak, 1 ½ - 2" thick
Coarse ground black pepper

- Sprinkle top side of steak generously with pepper. Press pepper into the meat with the palm of your hand. Turn and repeat on the other side. Let steak rest at room temperature for 1 hour.

- Place on the middle grill over medium heat. Turn only once.

Rare steak - 15-20 minutes each side

Medium - 25 minutes each side

Well done - 30 minutes, turn steak, reduce heat to medium-low for 35 minutes.

Note: If you are cooking a thin steak, 1" or less, use the lower grill.

Serves 4

Sirloin in Bacon

2 pounds beef top sirloin steak, 1 ½ - 2" thick
4 bacon slices

- Cut steak into 4 equal pieces. Wrap a bacon slice tightly around edge of each piece of steak and secure with toothpicks.
- Barbecue as for Sirloin au Poivre.
- Remove steaks to a platter and remove the toothpicks.

Serves 4

Minute or Cubed Steak

1 pound minute or cubed steak
2 - 3 tablespoons butter, melted
2 teaspoons lemon juice
1 teaspoon Worcestershire sauce

- Place the steaks on the lower grill over medium-low heat. Sprinkle the top side with pepper and cook for about 4 minutes. Turn and sprinkle top side with pepper, cooking for another 4 minutes.
- Place the steaks on open faced buttered buns, warmed on the upper rack for a couple of minutes. Pour over it a mixture of the melted butter, lemon juice and Worcestershire sauce.

Serves 2

Steak Marinade

This is excellent to use on less expensive cuts of meat, steak in particular, or ones that you are not too certain as to their degree of tenderness or flavor.
It may be bottled and stored in the refrigerator. It will last forever!

1 cup soya sauce
2 large onions, coarsely chopped
2 garlic cloves, halved
¼ cup bottled gravy colouring (Kitchen Bouquet)
2 teaspoons Beau Monde seasoning

- Combine soya sauce, onion and garlic in blender and process at high speed until smooth. Blend in gravy colouring and Beau Monde.
- Brush on steak and marinate for 2 hours.

Beef Tenderloin

1 - 4 pound beef tenderloin
Vegetable oil
Garlic cloves

Roasts should be 3 ½ to 4 pounds at least, so they will remain juicy and tender. Allow approximately ½ pound of tenderloin per person. Insert the spit rod through the centre of the tenderloin, lengthwise, and secure with holding forks.

- Place on the rotisserie over high indirect heat and brush all over with oil.
- Cook on high heat for a few minutes to seal in the juices.
- Reduce heat to medium and cook for approximately 15 minutes per pound for medium-rare.
- You may insert garlic cloves in slits in the meat or throw a few on the coals during the cooking process.
- Insert meat thermometer in the centre of the meat, being careful not to let it touch the spit.

Rare 140° F
Medium 160° F
Well done 170° F

- Be sure to let the roast rest for 15 minutes before carving to allow the meat to firm up.

Serves 6 to 8

Oriental Veal Cutlets

2 pounds veal cutlets
1 - 8 ounce can crushed pineapple
½ cup chopped water chestnuts
4 bacon slices
¼ cup olive oil

- Drain the pineapple and reserve the juice.
- Mix together the pineapple and water chestnuts. Spread the mixture on half of each veal cutlet.
- Roll up the veal and wrap in a slice of bacon, securing with toothpicks.
- Mix together the reserved pineapple juice and olive oil as a baste.
- Place the veal cutlets on the middle grill over medium heat. Brush with the baste and cook for 15 minutes, basting occasionally. Turn, cook for an additional 15 minutes, again, basting occasionally, until veal is tender.

Serves 4

Wine Basted Veal Chops

4 veal chops, 1 ½" thick

Wine Baste:
⅓ cup butter
2 tablespoons scallions, finely chopped
2 tablespoons dry white wine

- Cook the scallions in the butter for a few minutes, until tender. Remove from heat and add the wine.
- Place the veal chops on the middle grill over medium heat and baste with the mixture. Turn after 8 minutes, baste and cook for 8 more minutes.

Serves 4

lamb

Lamb

Lamb has been a neglected food for years and I am enjoying seeing its upsurge in popularity as it has long been one of our favorite foods. To properly enjoy lamb, avoid buying from the frozen food section of your grocery store. Instead, order fresh lamb from your butcher. It makes all the difference!

Lamb Burgers

1 pound ground lamb (not too lean)
1 teaspoon curry powder
½ teaspoon onion salt
½ teaspoon salt
¼ teaspoon pepper
1 egg
½ to ¾ cup dried bread crumbs

- Combine all the ingredients and shape into flat patties with your hands.
- Place on the middle grill over medium heat for 5 minutes on each side.
- Serve on buttered, toasted buns.

Note: a great way to use any leftover lamb mixture is to spoon it into scooped out zucchini halves and top with grated cheese. Wrap individually in aluminium foil and place on the middle grill over medium heat for 15 to 20 minutes.

Serves 4

Barbecued Lamb Shanks

4 meaty lamb shanks (3 pounds), cracked
¼ cup olive oil
½ cup dry sherry
¼ cup lemon juice
1 garlic clove, crushed
1 teaspoon crushed mint
½ teaspoon salt
¼ teaspoon pepper

- Place shanks in a large pot and cover with water. Simmer over medium heat until tender, about 30 minutes. Drain and return meat to pot. Let cool.
- Meanwhile, prepare marinade. Mix together the oil, sherry, lemon juice, garlic, mint, salt and pepper. Pour over the meat and toss to coat well. Cover and let marinate for 2 or 3 hours, turning and spooning marinade over meat frequently.
- Remove shanks from mixture and place on middle grill over medium heat. Heat the marinade on the barbecue. Cook for 20 to 25 minutes, basting occasionally with the reserved marinade and turning, until browned and tender.
- Serve the remaining marinade on the side (heated) to pour over the meat when served.

Serves 4

Souvlaki or Lamb Shish Kabob

2 pounds lean lamb, in 2 inch cubes
1 large onion, sliced and separated into rings
2 tablespoons olive oil
4 tablespoons lemon juice
½ tablespoon salt
½ teaspoon fresh ground pepper
2 tablespoons heavy cream

- Drop the onion rings into a deep bowl, sprinkle with olive oil, lemon juice, salt and pepper. Add the lamb, tossing to coat well. Marinate at room temperature for 2 hours, turning occasionally.
- Thread lamb tightly on six inch long metal skewers. Brush the meat evenly on all sides with the cream.
- Place on the lower grill over medium heat for 15 to 20 minutes, turning frequently, with the lid down.

"Kabob" is cube-shaped food threaded on a skewer, "shish".

Serves 6

Herbed Lamb Chops

¼ cup dry red wine
½ freshly squeezed lemon
¼ teaspoon thyme crushed
¼ teaspoon crushed oregano
¼ teaspoon rosemary leaves
½ teaspoon crushed mint leaves
4 large lamb chops, 1 inch thick

- In a small bowl, blend together the red wine, lemon juice and herbs.
- Place the lamb chops in the middle grill over medium heat and brush with the prepared herb sauce, generously. Cook for 10 minutes, basting frequently. Turn and cook for an additional 10 minutes, again, basting frequently.

Serves 4

Rack of Lamb

2 racks of lamb, 1½ - 2 pounds each, trimmed
2 garlic cloves, crushed
½ cup water
¼ cup dried mint leaves
¼ cup cider vinegar
¼ cup sugar

- Rub racks of lamb all over with the crushed garlic cloves. Wrap foil around the bone tips, shiny side out to reflect the heat. This prevents bones from charring and breaking.
- Place on the middle grill over medium-low heat for one hour, turning after 30 minutes.
- Meanwhile, bring the water and mint leaves to a boil and then simmer for 5 minutes, uncovered.
- Remove from heat and mix in the vinegar and sugar. Baste the lamb with this mixture for the last 20 minutes of cooking time.

Note: Place a foil drip pan under the meat if flare-ups occur.

Serves 4

Lamb Shoulder

1 4-5 pound shoulder of lamb
½ teaspoon salt
¼ teaspoon pepper
½ teaspoon garlic powder
½ teaspoon crushed mint leaves
½ teaspoon oregano

- Insert the spit rod through the centre of the shoulder of lamb, balancing carefully and securing with holding forks.
- Combine the salt, pepper, garlic, mint and oregano. Rub this mixture well into the meat.
- Place on the rotisserie over medium indirect heat for approximately 2 to 2 ½ hours, until the meat thermometer registers 170 ° F for medium or 180 ° F for well done.

Let rest 10 minutes before carving.

Serves 6 to 8

Stuffed Leg of Lamb

1 - 5 pound leg of lamb, boned for stuffing
3 or 4 garlic cloves
¼ cup butter
1 small onion, finely chopped
½ cup chopped celery
2 cups soft bread crumbs
¼ cup chopped parsley
1 teaspoon dried mint leaves
½ teaspoon salt
Dash of pepper
1 tablespoon lemon or lime juice

1 lemon
½ teaspoon salt
¼ teaspoon pepper
1 teaspoon crushed rosemary

- Trim any excess fat, if necessary, from the lamb. Cut 5 or 6 small slits in the fat of the lamb and insert slivers of garlic. Set aside.
- Prepare the stuffing. In a small skillet, melt the butter and cook the chopped onion and celery until just soft. Remove from heat and mix in a bowl with the bread crumbs, parsley, mint, salt, pepper and lemon juice. Stuff the mixture into the pocket of the lamb, packing well. Pull together and tie securely every 2 inches with strong string.
- Insert the spit, lengthwise, through the leg of lamb, balancing carefully. Secure with holding forks. Rub the lamb all over with lemon halves. Mix together the salt, pepper and rosemary and rub into the outside of the lamb.
- Place on the rotisserie and barbecue over medium indirect heat for approximately 2 ½ hours, until golden brown and the thermometer registers 170 ° F for medium or 180 ° F for well done. Remove garlic slivers and let rest for 10 minutes before carving.

Serves 6 to 8

pork

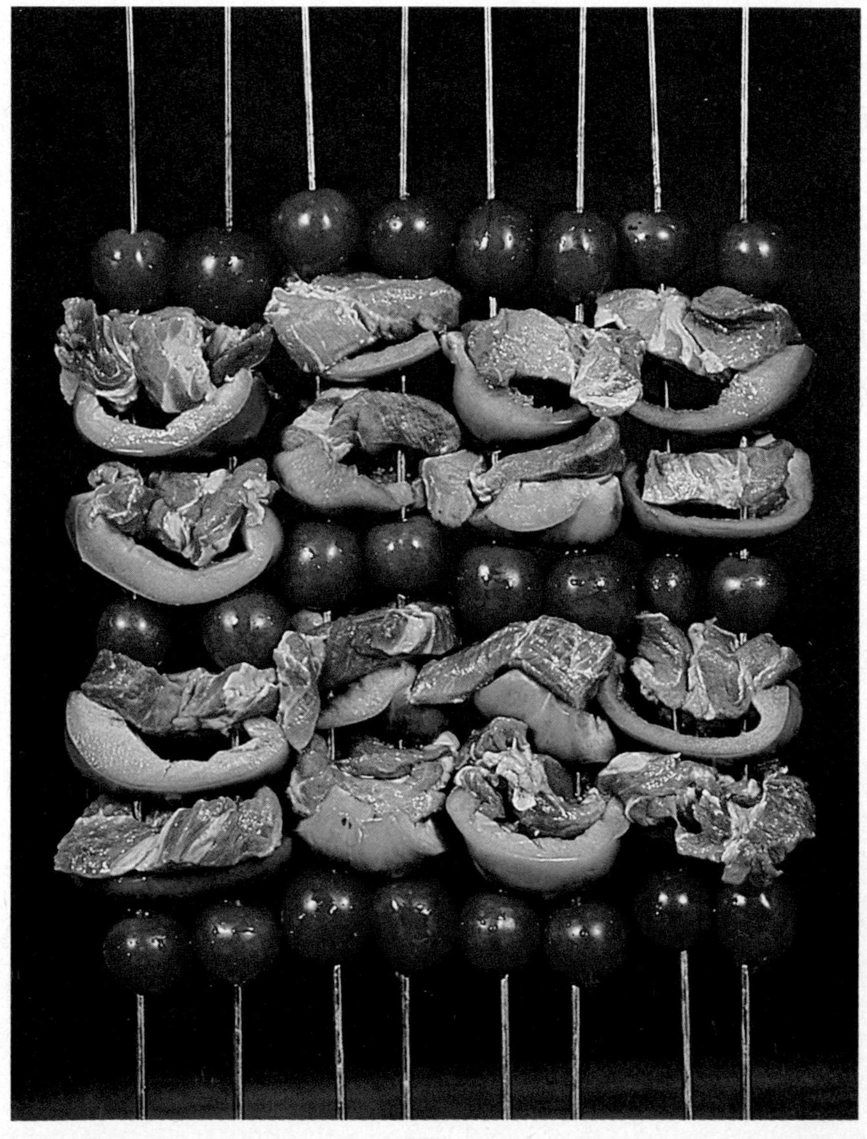

Pork

Some tips about cooking pork. Be sure to trim excess fat to prevent "flare-ups" as they are most common with pork. Use slow cooking to assure your meat is cooked all the way through. Make sure all pinkness is gone but don't cook any longer or your meat may dry out. A meat thermometer is a necessary tool and the most accurate.

Hawaiian Pork Chops

4 large, ½ inch thick pork chops
4 pineapple rings
4 teaspoons brown sugar
4 maraschino cherries

- Lay the pork chops on a double layer of aluminium foil to prevent flare-up from the drippings. Place on the middle grill over high heat for 15 minutes, until browned. Turn and lay a pineapple ring on top of each chop. Place a teaspoon of brown sugar in each pineapple hole and top with a cherry. Cook for an additional 10 or 15 minutes.

Serves 4

Cheese'n Bacon Dogs

- Slit weiners lengthwise, not quite all the way through. Insert a thin strip of Cheddar cheese in each slit and wrap each weiner in a strip of bacon, securing with toothpicks on each end.
- Place on the upper rack over medium heat for 5 minutes or until the bacon is crisp. Serve on toasted, buttered buns.

Spiced Pork Kabobs

½ cup vegetable oil
½ cup orange juice
¼ cup cider vinegar
1 small onion, in ¼ inch slices
1 teaspoon salt
¼ teaspoon pepper
3 garlic cloves, crushed
½ teaspoon marjoram
2 pounds lean pork shoulder or loin

- In a large bowl mix together the first 8 ingredients. Cut the pork into 1 inch cubes and add to the marinade, tossing to coat well. Cover and refrigerate for four hours. Drain, reserving the marinade.
- Thread the meat onto 6 long metal skewers (18 inches), ¼ inch apart to assure complete cooking all the way through.
- Place on the lower grill over medium heat with the lid down for 40 minutes, turning and basting with the reserved marinade occasionally.

Serves 6

Luau Spareribs

3 - 4 pounds pork spareribs
1/3 cup sugar
2 1/2 tablespoons cornstarch
1/2 teaspoon ground ginger
1 teaspoon salt
1/4 teaspoon pepper
2/3 cup water
1/3 cup lemon juice
1/4 cup soya sauce
1/4 cup Worcestershire sauce

- In a small saucepan, mix sugar, cornstarch, ginger, salt and pepper. Stir in water, lemon juice, soya sauce and Worcestershire sauce. Cook over moderate heat, stirring constantly, until it thickens. Brush meat with light coatings of the glaze while barbecuing.

Serves 4

Country Ribs

4 pounds pork country ribs, cut into 2 rib portions
1 cup unsweetened grapefruit juice
1/2 cup brown sugar
3 teaspoons cornstarch
1 teaspoon salt
1 teaspoon curry powder
1/2 teaspoon ground allspice

- In medium saucepan, over moderate heat, combine all the ingredients, except the ribs, and bring to a boil. Stir constantly for one minute. Remove from heat.
- Brush ribs frequently with this mixture while barbecuing.

Serves 4

Celebrity Glazed Pork Roast

4 pounds boneless pork loin roast, rolled and tied
1 teaspoon salt
½ teaspoon pepper
½ teaspoon garlic salt
1 cup catsup
½ cup applesauce
1 tablespoon vinegar
Dash of cayenne

- Mix together in a small bowl, the salt, pepper and garlic salt. Rub well into the pork roast.
- Place the roast on rotisserie over medium heat for about 2 hours or until a meat thermometer inserted in the centre registers 180 ° F. Do not leave the thermometer in the meat while cooking as, on the barbecue, it will give you a false reading.
- Meanwhile, in a small saucepan, combine the catsup, applesauce, vinegar and cayenne. Bring to a boil, then simmer, uncovered, for 5 minutes. Let cool.
- Approximately 15 minutes before the roast is done, brush generously with applesauce mixture.

Serves 6 to 8

Stuffed Pork Leg Roast

2 medium apples, peeled, cored, finely chopped
3 tablespoons brown sugar
1 teaspoon lemon juice
1 4 - 5 pound pork leg roast, boned

Baste:
6 ounces frozen orange juice concentrate, thawed
2 tablespoons brown sugar
¼ teaspoon ground cloves

- In a small bowl, mix together the apple, brown sugar and lemon juice. Stuff this into the cavity of the roast. Pull in the sides and close tightly with small skewers or tie with heavy string.
- Insert the spit rod through the centre of the roast, balancing carefully and securing with holding forks. Place on the rotisserie over low heat with a foil drip pan underneath.
- Cook for 3 to 3 ½ hours until meat thermometer registers 185 ° F and meat is no longer pink in the centre.
- Prepare the baste. Mix together well and use to baste for the last hour of cooking time.

Serves 6 to 8

Ham Steak with Mustard Sauce

½ cup maple syrup or corn syrup
1 teaspoon dry mustard
1 tablespoon brown sugar
1 - 2 pound ham steak, 1 inch thick

- In a small bowl, mix together the syrup, mustard and brown sugar. Slash the edges of the ham to prevent curling. Place on the middle grill over medium heat, brushing occasionally with the mustard sauce. Cook 8 minutes on each side, turning just once. If cooking too fast, lift lid slightly.
- Remove from heat to platter and brush again with sauce.

Serves 4

Apricot Glazed Ham

4 - 5 pound smoked ham
Whole cloves
12 - 15 dried apricots
¾ cup brown sugar
1 teaspoon dry mustard

- Score the fat surface of the ham in diagonal shapes. Insert cloves in the cross-sections of the diamond shapes.
- Place the ham on the rotisserie, securing tightly with holding forks and balancing carefully. Cook over low heat, 300 ° F for about two hours, with the lid down. If you have a two-burner barbecue, turn only the one side on, using indirect heat.
- Meanwhile, prepare the glaze. Place the apricots in a small saucepan, barely covered with water and simmer for 20 minutes, covered. Drain the apricots and puree in food processor. Blend in the brown sugar and dry mustard.
- Apply this glaze to the ham and cook for an additional 30 minutes.

Serves 8 to 10

seafood

Seafood

There are so many wonderful things you can do with fish and seafood, and with added benefits for the diet conscious! It is a nice change from red meat so I make sure to insert it in my menus regularly. It is also the perfect light food for those hot summer days.

Looney Tuna Burgers

1 pound zucchini (2 medium-sized)
1 small onion
14 ounces of canned tuna, drained and flaked
1 egg
½ teaspoon salt
¼ teaspoon pepper
¼ cup mayonnaise
3 cups fresh bread crumbs
1 tablespoon vegetable oil

- Cut the ends from the zucchini and grate the zucchini finely with a vegetable grater. Remove all the excess moisture by squeezing in a towel. Grate the onion finely. Mix together in a medium-size bowl and add the flaked tuna, egg, salt, pepper, mayonnaise, bread crumbs and vegetable oil.
- Shape the mixture into large patties and place on the lower grill over high heat, with the lid down, for 10 minutes. Turn and cook for an additional 10 minutes, until golden brown on both sides.
- Place on toasted hamburger buns and garnish with lettuce, tomato slices and mayonnaise.

Serves 6 to 8

Toasting Buns
Open buns and butter both sides well. Place face down on middle grill over medium heat for a couple of minutes, until lightly toasted.

Fillets in Caper Sauce

2 pounds fish fillets (Sole, Boston Bluefish, Turbot)
¼ cup melted butter
¼ cup mayonnaise
1 tablespoon lemon juice
1 tablespoon capers
1 tablespoon chopped parsley
Dash of pepper

- Lay the fish on a large sheet of heavy-duty aluminium foil (or double-thickness of regular).
- Mix together the remaining ingredients and pour over the fish. Seal securely.
- Place on the middle grill over low heat for 20 to 25 minutes, until the fish flakes easily with a fork.

Fish in Corn Husks

4 corn husks
2 pounds fish fillets
Butter
Lemon juice
Salt and Pepper
Dried Dill weed (optional)
Capers (optional)

- Remove corn cob and silk from husks, carefully, leaving husks intact. Soak husks in water for a few minutes if they are dry.
- Place one or two fish fillets (depending on the size) in each corn husk. Smear the fillets with butter and sprinkle with lemon juice, salt and pepper. You may also sprinkle with dill weed and/or a few capers. Bring the husks together, enclosing the fish completely and tightly. Tie the silk ends of the husks together with wet string.
- Place on the middle grill, seam side up, over medium heat, for about 20 minutes. May be served in the husks to be decorative, or remove them from the husks.

Serves 4

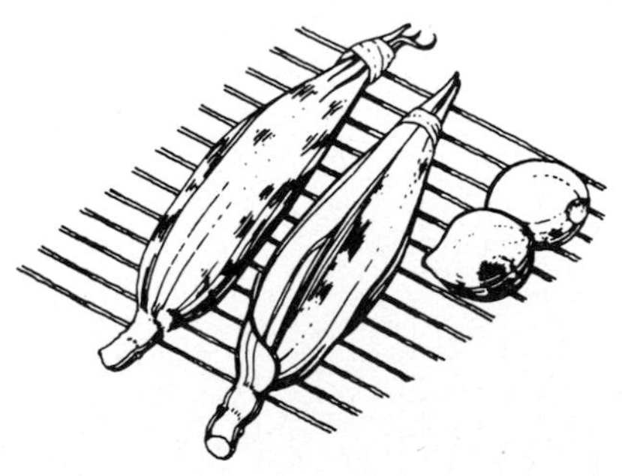

Red Snapper

2 pounds Red Snapper fillets, ¾ to 1" thick
½ cup tomato juice
1 tablespoon vegetable oil
2 tablespoons lemon juice
½ teaspoon salt
1 garlic clove, crushed
1 teaspoon fennel seed
1 teaspoon ginger

- Place the snapper fillets in a shallow pan.
- Mix together the remaining ingredients and pour over the fish. Marinate for 2 hours in refrigerator. Drain, reserving the marinade.
- Place on the middle grill over medium heat for 12 - 15 minutes, brushing occasionally and turning once.
- You may also simply place the fillets on the middle grill over medium heat for 12 - 15 minutes, turning and brushing with any of the prepared butters on pages 120, 121.

Serves 4

Piquant Fish Steaks

2 pounds fish steaks, ½ - ¾" thick (Cod, Flounder, Halibut, Swordfish)
½ cup vegetable oil
¼ cup lemon juice
½ teaspoon salt
Dash white pepper
1 tablespoon chopped parsley
¼ teaspoon dry mustard
1 teaspoon dried chervil

- Lay the steaks in a shallow pan.
- Mix together the remaining ingredients for the marinade. Pour over the fish, coating evenly.
- Marinate in refrigerator for 2 hours. Drain, reserving the marinade.
- Place steaks on the middle grill over medium heat for 8 - 10 minutes on each side, turning once and brushing with the reserved marinade.

Serves 4

Simple Salmon Steak

½ cup lemon juice
2 tablespoons vegetable oil
½ teaspoon salt
1 teaspoon paprika
1 tablespoon chopped chives
1 teaspoon dried dill weed
1 ½ pounds salmon steaks, (4) 1 inch thick

- In a small bowl, combine the first 6 ingredients. Lay the salmon steaks in a shallow pan and pour the mixture over it. Marinate in refrigerator for one hour.
- Remove the steak, reserving the marinade for basting. Lay the steaks on the middle grill over medium heat (300 ° F) for 5 to 7 minutes, (lid down) brushing a few times with the marinade. Turn and cook for an additional 5 to 7 minutes, again brushing with the marinade, until the fish flakes easily.

Serves 4

Stuffed Whole Salmon

3 pounds whole salmon, dressed
3 tablespoons butter
1 small onion, finely chopped
½ cup chopped celery
½ teaspoon salt
2 teaspoons grated lemon peel
½ teaspoon dried dill weed
¼ cup sour cream
3 cups soft bread crumbs

- Rinse fish under cold running water and dry with paper towel.
- Prepare the stuffing: Melt the butter in a small skillet and add the onion and celery, cooking over medium heat until tender (5 min.). Remove from heat and blend in the salt, lemon peel, dill and sour cream. Mix in the bread crumbs. Spoon the stuffing into the cavity of the salmon.
- Close the cavity by inserting skewers or toothpicks at 1'' intervals. Secure by lacing together with strong string. Rub the fish with oil.
- Place on a sheet of foil on the middle grill over medium heat, with the lid lowered, not closed. You may also place the salmon in a fish basket on the rotisserie.

Serves 4

Cooking Times
1 - 1 ½ pounds - 10 min. each side
2 - 3 pounds - 15 min. each side
4 - 5 pounds - 20 min. each side

Fish is done when it flakes easily with a fork. Serve with juice from the foil package.

Fish with Sour Cream Stuffing

2 pounds fish fillets (Sole, Flounder, Swordfish, Haddock, Halibut)
2 tablespoons butter
1 small onion, finely chopped
¼ cup chopped celery
½ teaspoon salt
Dash pepper
¼ cup sour cream
2 tablespoons chopped parsley
1 teaspoon dried chervil
2 cups soft bread crumbs

- Pat the fish fillets dry with paper towel. Melt the butter in a small skillet and cook the onions until tender. Pour into a medium bowl and add the remaining ingredients, mixing well.
- Lay the fish fillets out on the counter and spread the stuffing over the fillets, leaving a one-inch border all around. Roll up, jelly-roll fashion, and secure every inch with wooden toothpicks. If necessary, lace in between the toothpicks with heavy string.
- Oil lightly and place in hinged grill basket, on rotisserie, over medium heat for 20 minutes.

Serves 4

Stuffed Trout

2 whole Trout, 1 - 1 ½ pounds each
2 cups soft bread crumbs
1 small onion, finely chopped
4 tablespoons melted butter
½ teaspoon salt
¼ teaspoon pepper
1 egg, beaten
1 tablespoon chopped pimento
1 tablespoon chopped parsley

- Wash the fish under cold running water. Drain well. Mix the remaining ingredients together to prepare the stuffing. Spoon half the stuffing into each fish.
- Pull fish together and insert wooden toothpicks or short skewers every inch. Lace in between the toothpicks with heavy string, pulling fish tightly together.
- Brush the fish with oil and place in hinged grill basket. Insert spit rod and place on rotisserie over medium heat, with the lid up slightly, for 25 minutes, until fish flakes easily with a fork.
- If you do not have a grill basket, you may place the trout on the middle grill over medium heat for 25 minutes.
- Garnish with lemon wedges.

Serves 4

Smoked Fish

You may use basically any kind of whole fish or fillets, a couple of pounds or 5 pounds. You may have to increase the cooking time as you increase the amount of fish to be smoked.

- Soak one or two cups of hickory chips (depends on the amount of fish to be smoked) in water for at least one hour. Thaw fish if frozen.
- Place the fish in an oiled grill basket on the rotisserie, over low heat, with the hood down.
- Place half of the chips on the lava rocks or in a smoker unit. Add more chips as needed.
- Smoke for ½ an hour for 1 - 2 pounds of fish at 150 ° - 170 ° F. Baste with oil as needed.
- It is done when the fish is golden and flakes easily with a fork.
- Skin and bone the fish and lay out on a platter. May be served warm or cold. See page 23 for a recipe for Smoked Fish Spread.

Sesame Scallops

1 pound scallops
¼ cup pineapple juice
¼ cup sherry
Melted butter
Sesame seeds

- Rinse the scallops under cold running water and drain well. Mix together the pineapple juice and sherry in a small bowl and add the scallops. Marinate for one or two hours.
- Drain the scallops and thread onto 6 inch wooden skewers. Brush with melted butter and roll in the sesame seeds.
- Place on the middle grill over medium heat for 5 minutes, turning frequently.

Serves 4

Shrimp and Artichoke Hearts

1 or 2 pounds shrimp
14 ounce can artichoke hearts
¼ cup lemon juice
2 tablespoons cider vinegar
¼ cup vegetable oil
½ teaspoon salt
1 teaspoon Worcestershire sauce
¼ teaspoon garlic powder
¼ teaspoon crushed oregano

- Wash the shrimp in cold water and drain well. Drain the artichoke hearts. In a medium-sized bowl, combine the remaining ingredients. Add the shrimp and artichoke hearts and marinate in refrigerator for two hours.
- Thread the shrimp on skewers, lengthwise, through the centre, making the heads double up against the tails. Alternate with the artichoke hearts.
- Place on the middle grill over medium heat for 5 minutes, turning once.

Ginger Shrimp

1 pound shrimp
¾ cup sherry
¼ cup soya sauce
1 teaspoon sugar
½ teaspoon ground ginger

- Wash the shrimp in cold water and drain well. Pat dry with paper towel. Thread the shrimp onto 6 inch wooden skewers, lengthwise, through the centre, making heads double up against tails. Lay on a platter.
- Mix together the remaining ingredients and brush generously all over the shrimp. Refrigerate for one hour.
- Place the skewered shrimp on the middle grill over medium heat for 5 minutes, turning once.

Seafood Kabobs

1 pound shrimp
1 pound scallops
¼ cup soya sauce
¼ cup vegetable oil
¼ cup lemon juice
¼ cup chopped parsley
½ teaspoon salt
¼ teaspoon pepper

- Wash the shrimp and scallops in cold water and drain well. Mix together the remaining ingredients in a medium-sized bowl and add the shrimp and scallops. Marinate in refrigerator for one hour. Drain and thread alternately on skewers.
- Place on middle grill over medium heat for 5 minutes, turning once.
- With the seafood kabobs, you may also add to the skewers, cherry tomatoes, olives, pickles, mushroom caps or pineapple chunks.

Herbed Shrimp

3 pounds shrimp
½ cup melted butter
2 tablespoons lemon juice
¼ cup chopped parsley
1 small onion, finely chopped
½ teaspoon salt
1 garlic clove, minced
½ teaspoon Worcestershire sauce

- Wash the shrimp in cold water and drain well. Pat dry with paper towel. Mix together the remaining ingredients and then add the shrimp.
- Spoon the mixture onto a large sheet of heavy-duty aluminium foil and seal securely.
- Place the foil package on the middle grill over medium heat for 15 minutes.

Hint: Estimate a half a pound of seafood per person.

Serves 6

Grilled Whole Lobster

1 to 1 ½ pounds lobster person

Stuffing:
2 tablespoons dried bread crumbs
1 teaspoon lemon juice

Basting Sauce:
½ cup melted butter
¼ cup lemon juice
½ teaspoon salt
2 tablespoons chopped parsley
¼ teaspoon garlic powder
or 1 small clove, minced

To Prepare Live Lobster:

- With a sharp knife, sever the vein at the base of the neck, underneath the shell. Place the lobster on his back and, with your hand wrapped in a towel, hold him firmly in place by the head. Draw the knife from the head, down through the abdomen, thus allowing the lobster to lie flat and evenly expose the meat. Remove the stomach (hard sac near the head) and the intestine that runs from it through the middle of the abdomen to the tail. Discard.

- Remove the red coral and the green liver or tomalley. Place these in a small bowl and mix together with the bread crumbs and lemon juice. Replace in the cavity.

- Combine the butter, lemon juice, salt, parsley and garlic. Brush on the lobster meat and place in a hinged wire basket.

- Place the basket on the middle grill over medium heat, shell-side up, for 8 to 10 minutes. Turn and grill for an additional 8 minutes until lightly browned and tender. Before serving, brush again with the basting sauce. Serve the remainder on the side for dipping.

- Be careful not to overcook as it will toughen the meat and ruin the flavour.

King Crab Legs

2 pounds King crab legs
½ cup butter
¼ cup lemon juice
¼ cup dry white wine
1 tablespoon finely chopped scallions or chives

- Prepare the butter dip by melting the butter in a small saucepan and adding the lemon juice, wine and scallions or chives. Cook over low heat for a couple of minutes. Keep warm.
- Place the crab legs on the middle grill over low heat for approximately 15 minutes, turning once.
- Serve with the hot dipping sauce on the side in individual serving dishes. Be sure to supply claw crackers and seafood forks.

Serves 4

Frogs Legs Provençal

½ cup dry white wine
¼ cup vegetable oil
¼ teaspoon salt
⅛ teaspoon pepper
½ teaspoon crushed thyme
1 garlic clove, crushed
2 pounds frogs legs

- Mix together the first 6 ingredients in your blender.
- Place the frogs legs in a shallow pan and pour the marinade over them. Marinate for 2 hours, turning occasionally.
- Drain well and reserve the marinade
- Place the frogs legs on the middle grill over medium heat and brush frequently with the reserved marinade. Turn after about 5 minutes, when they are golden brown, and cook for an additional 5 minutes.

Serves 4

vegetables

Vegetables

A lot of people are cooking their meat dishes on the barbecue but still insist on doing their vegetables indoors. Why heat up your kitchen and end up standing over a hot stove until dinner is served? You won't be sacrificing quality as grilling in foil blends all the flavours and proper timing will guarantee everything is cooked to perfection.

Hash Browns

4 large potatoes
2 scallions, finely chopped
½ teaspoon salt
¼ teaspoon pepper
1 ½ teaspoon paprika
Dash of garlic salt
2 teaspoons toasted sesame seeds (optional)
2 tablespoons butter

- Scrub the potatoes and dice. Place in a medium-sized bowl and toss with the scallions, salt, pepper, paprika, garlic salt and sesame seeds.
- Lay the mixture on a double-thickness of foil or a single-thickness of heavy-duty foil, 18" x 12". Dot with the butter and seal securely.
- Place on the middle grill over medium heat for 20 minutes, until fork tender.

Serves 4

Baked Potatoes

- Scrub baking potatoes and puncture a few times with a fork.
- Place on the upper rack over medium heat for approximately 60 minutes with the lid down. Cooking time will differ according to the size of the potatoes.

  I find that by wrapping the potatoes in aluminium foil, the cooking time is reduced. Medium-sized potatoes will take approximately 40 minutes.

  Baked potatoes often take longer to cook than most other barbecue dishes so it is a good idea to put them on immediately after preheating the barbecue.

Au Gratin Potatoes

4 large baking potatoes
Salt
Pepper
Chopped chives
Grated Mozzarella cheese
2 tablespoons butter

- Scrub the potatoes and cut into ¼-inch wide slices. Lay half of the slices out on a 20'' x 12'' sheet of aluminium foil. Sprinkle with salt, pepper, chopped chives and grated cheese. Top with remaining half of potato slices and dot with butter. Bring up ends of foil and seal securely.
- Place the foil package on the middle grill over medium heat for 30 minutes, or until the potatoes are fork tender.

Serves 4

Potato Cakes

4 medium-sized potatoes
4 scallions, chopped
¾ teaspoon salt
¼ teaspoon pepper
½ teaspoon Worcestershire sauce
2 eggs
¼ pound bacon pieces

- Boil the peeled potatoes until soft. Drain and place in a medium-sized bowl. Mash together with the scallions, salt, pepper, Worcestershire, and eggs. Fry the bacon pieces and add them and their drippings to the mixture. Blend together thoroughly. Shape with your hands into patties.
- Place on the middle grill over medium heat for 5 minutes or until browned on the bottom side. Turn and cook for an additional 5 minutes until browned.

Serves 4

Potatoes and Onions

4 medium potatoes
1 small onion
Salt and pepper
1 tablespoon chives
3 tablespoons butter

- Wash and scrub the potatoes. Cut into ¼ inch thick slices and lay half of the potato slices on a double-thickness of aluminium foil, 18'' x 12''. slice the onion thinly and lay on top of the potatoes. Sprinkle with the salt, pepper and chives and dot with the butter. Lay the rest of the potatoes on top. Bring the long sides of the foil together and fold over twice, sealing securely. Fold in the ends tightly.
- Lay the foil package on the middle grill over medium heat for 20 minutes or until the potatoes are fork-tender.

The onions steam flavour right through the potatoes.

Serves 4

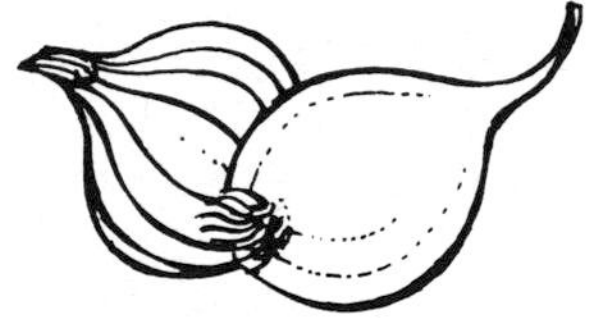

Vegetable Rice

2 ¼ cups water
2 ¼ cups precooked rice
1 small onion, finely chopped
1 tablespoon pimento, finely chopped
3 tablespoons green pepper, finely chopped
1 small tomato, finely chopped
1 small carrot, finely chopped
1 teaspoon salt
¼ teaspoon pepper
1 tablespoon chopped parsley
1 tablespoon butter

- Cut two 18'' x 12'' sheets of aluminium foil and press tightly inside a 1 ½ quart bowl or casserole dish.
- Bring the water to a boil. Remove from heat and add the rice and remaining ingredients. Mix well and spoon into the foil-lined dish. Carefully bring the ends of the foil together and secure tightly. Remove the package from the bowl.
- Place on the upper rack over medium heat for 10 minutes. Remove from heat, fluff up rice with a fork and serve immediately.

Serves 6

Mushroom Rice

2 cups water
1 cup finely chopped fresh mushrooms
1 tablespoon finely chopped onion
1 teaspoon salt
¼ teaspoon pepper
1 tablespoon Worcestershire sauce
2 tablespoons butter
¼ cup chopped parsley
2 cups pre-cooked rice
1 tablespoon chopped pimento

- Put the water on to boil and add the mushrooms, onion, salt, pepper, Worcestershire, butter and parsley. Boil for 2 or 3 minutes.
- Line a 1 ½-quart casserole dish with two sheets of aluminium foil, each 18'' x 12'', molding well.
- Remove the water from the heat and add the rice, mixing well. Let set for a couple of minutes, then pour into the foil-lined dish. Mix in the chopped pimento. Carefully fold over the sides of the foil and seal securely.
- Remove foil and mixture from dish and place on the middle grill over medium heat for 5 minutes.

Serves 6

Curried Rice

2 cups water
1 teaspoon salt
¼ teaspoon pepper
2 tablespoons chopped parsley
1 tablespoon butter
1 teaspoon curry powder
2 cups pre-cooked rice

- Bring the water and the next five ingredients to a boil. Stir in the rice and let set for a couple of minutes to absorb some of the water.
- Line a 1 ½ quart casserole dish with 2 sheets of aluminium foil, each 18'' x 12'', molding well into the dish. Pour the rice mixture into the foil-lined dish, bring up the sides and seal securely.
- Remove foil and mixture from dish and place on the upper rack over medium heat for 5 minutes.

Serves 6

Vegetable Kabobs

18 whole mushrooms
1 medium zucchini, in ½ inch slices
3 firm tomatoes, each cut in six wedges
or 18 cherry tomatoes
2 large peppers, cut in large pieces
12 small potatoes

Marinade:
½ cup vegetable oil
½ cup cider vinegar
3 teaspoons sugar
1 teaspoon salt
2 teaspoons tarragon leaves

- Prepare the vegetables. Par boil the potatoes, carefully, so that they are not too soft. Drain and cool in the refrigerator. In a medium-sized bowl, mix together the marinade ingredients. Add the vegetables and marinate for 2 hours, covered, in the refrigerator.
- Drain the vegetables and thread onto 6 long metal skewers, alternately.
- Place on the lower grill over low heat for about 5 minutes, until the vegetables are tender-crisp.

Serves 6

Vegetable Medley

2 large carrots, sliced
1 small zucchini, sliced
1 cup Brussel Sprouts
1 cup peas
2 ribs of celery, sliced
1 cup yellow wax beans, in 1 inch pieces
2 scallions chopped

- Use any four of the vegetables plus the scallions. You may add a vegetable for each additional person being served. Lay the vegetables on an 18'' x 12'' sheet of aluminium foil. Sprinkle with salt and pepper and dot with a couple of tablespoons of butter. Bring up the ends of the foil and seal securely.
- Place on the middle grill over medium heat for 20 minutes.

Serves 4

Broccoli

- Break a head of broccoli into flowerets and lay on an 18'' x 12'' sheet of aluminium foil. Sprinkle with salt and pepper and dot with 2 tablespoons of butter. Bring up ends of foil and seal securely.
- Place on the middle grill over medium heat for 10 minutes, until tender-crisp.

Serves 4

Dilled Wax Beans

1 pound yellow wax beans
Salt
Pepper
½ teaspoon dried dill weed
2 tablespoons butter

- Cut the beans into two-inch pieces and lay on a sheet of aluminium foil, 18'' x 12''. Sprinkle with salt, pepper and dill and dot with the butter. Bring up the ends of the foil and seal securely.
- Place on the upper rack over medium heat for 30 minutes or on the middle rack over medium heat for 15 to 20 minutes.

Serves 4

Courtney Carrots

4 medium-sized carrots
Salt
Pepper
1 teaspoon sugar
2 tablespoons butter

- Wash and scrape the carrots. Slice thinly (⅛ inch) and lay on a sheet of aluminium foil 18'' x 12''. Sprinkle with salt, pepper and sugar and dot with the butter. Bring up ends of foil and seal securely.
- Place on the middle grill over medium heat for about 8 minutes, until tender-crisp.

Serves 4

Whole Onions

- Thread 4 medium-sized, skinned onions on an 18'' long metal skewer. Brush with melted butter and sprinkle with salt and pepper.
- Place on the lower grill over medium heat for 10 minutes, turning frequently.

Serves 4

Sliced Onions

- Skin and cut 2 or 3 large onions in ¼ inch slices. Lay on a sheet of aluminium foil, 18'' x 12''. Sprinkle with salt and pepper and dot with a couple of tablespoons of butter. Seal securely.
- Place on the middle grill over medium heat for 20 minutes.

Serves 4

Sherry Mushrooms

¾ - 1 pound fresh mushrooms
Salt
Pepper
2 tablespoons butter
2 tablespoons sherry

- Wash and drain the mushrooms. Slice and lay on an 18'' x 12'' sheet of aluminium foil. Sprinkle with salt and pepper, dot with butter and drizzle the sherry over top. Seal securely.
- Place on the lower grill over low heat for 30 minutes or the middle grill over medium heat for 20 minutes.

Serves 4

Rosemary Cauliflower

1 small head cauliflower
2 scallions, chopped
Salt
Pepper
1 teaspoon rosemary leaves
2 tablespoons butter

- Break the cauliflower into flowerets. Place on a sheet of aluminium foil, 18'' x 12''. Sprinkle with the chopped scallions, salt, pepper and rosemary leaves. Dot with the butter and bring up sides of foil, folding together and sealing securely.
- Lay the foil package on the middle grill over medium heat for 10 to 15 minutes, until tender-crisp.

Serves 4

Dilled Cauliflower

1 small head cauliflower
Salt
Pepper
1 teaspoon dried dill weed
2 tablespoons butter

- Divide the cauliflower into flowerets. Place on a sheet of aluminium foil, 18'' x 12''. Sprinkle with salt, pepper and dried dill weed and dab with the butter. Bring up the sides of the foil and seal securely.
- Place on the middle grill over medium heat for 10 to 15 minutes, until tender-crisp.

Serves 4

Cauliflower and Peas

1 head cauliflower
1 cup frozen peas
Salt
Pepper
Mozzarella cheese
2 tablespoons butter

- Divide the cauliflower into flowerets and lay half of it on a double-thickness of aluminium foil, 18'' x 12''. Place ½ cup of frozen peas on top. Sprinkle with salt and pepper and lay slices of mozzarella cheese on top of this. Top with the remaining cauliflower and ½ cup of peas, sprinkle with salt and pepper and dot with butter. Bring up ends of foil and seal securely.
- Place on the middle grill over medium heat for 10 minutes, until the cheese melts and the cauliflower is tender-crisp.

Serves 4

Brussel Sprouts

1 pound brussel sprouts
Salt
Pepper
Lemon Juice
2 tablespoons butter

- Cut the stem ends from the sprouts and lay on a sheet of aluminium foil, 18" x 12". Sprinkle with salt, pepper and a bit of lemon juice and dot with the butter. Bring up ends of foil and seal securely.
- Place on the middle grill over medium heat for 10 minutes, or until easily pierced with a fork.

Serves 4

Stuffed Tomatoes

2 large, firm tomatoes
Salt
Crushed oregano
Grated Mozzarella or Cheddar cheese
Buttered bread crumbs

- Cut the tomatoes in half and scoop out the seeds from in between the spokes. Sprinkle the cavities with salt and oregano and fill with grated cheese, packing it in. Top with the buttered bread crumbs.
- Place on the upper rack over low heat for 20 to 25 minutes, until heated through and cheese has melted.

Serves 4

Green Tomatoes

2 or 3 large green tomatoes
Butter
Salt
Pepper
Basil or thyme
Grated Parmesan cheese

- Slice the tomatoes ¼ inch thick. Spread half the tomato slices with a bit of butter and sprinkle with salt, pepper, a bit of crushed basil or thyme and Parmesan. Sandwich the rest of the slices on top. Lay a sheet of aluminium foil, 18'' x 12'', and seal securely.
- Place on the middle grill over medium heat for 10 minutes.

Serves 4

Stuffed Green Peppers

4 firm green peppers
1 ½ cup cooked rice (when cooked equals 3 cups)
1 large tomato, chopped
1 tablespoon chopped pimento
1 tablespoon finely chopped onion
½ teaspoon salt
¼ teaspoon pepper
½ teaspoon crushed basil
½ cup grated cheese (Mozzarella or Cheddar)

- Slice off the top of the stem end of each pepper and remove seeds and white ribs. Place each pepper, cut side up, on a double-thickness of aluminium foil.
- In a medium-sized bowl, mix together the cooked rice, tomato, pimento, onion, salt, pepper and basil. Stuff the peppers with this mixture and place grated cheese on top. Bring up the sides of the foil and wrap securely.
- Place on the middle grill over medium heat for 15 minutes.

Serves 4

Green Vegies

1 small zucchini, in ¼-inch slices
1 cup brussel sprouts
2 cups broccoli, broken into flowerets
Salt
Lemon pepper or black pepper
Crushed Tarragon leaves
2 tablespoons butter

- Lay the vegetables on an 18" x 12" sheet of aluminium foil. Sprinkle with the salt, pepper, tarragon and dot with butter. Bring up ends of foil and seal securely.
- Place on the middle grill over medium heat for 20 minutes.

Serves 4

Stuffed Zucchini

4 medium-sized zucchini (2 pounds)
½ pound ground beef
¼ cup mayonnaise
2 tablespoons finely chopped onion
1 tablespoon chopped parsley
1 teaspoon salt
¼ teaspoon pepper
Dash of ground cayenne
1 cup grated Mozzarella cheese

- Slice each zucchini in half, lengthwise, and scoop out the centres, leaving about ¼ inch of shell. A serrated grapefruit spoon works well.
- Chop up the zucchini from the centres and mix with the ground beef, mayonnaise, onion, parsley, salt, pepper and cayenne. Spoon into the zucchini shells and top with the grated cheese.
- Wrap individually in aluminium foil, loosely, but securing ends by twisting.
- Place foil packets on the middle grill over medium heat for 15 to 20 minutes.

Serves 4

Sliced Zucchini

- Cut 2 medium-sized zucchini into ¼-inch thick slices. Lay on a double thickness of aluminium foil, 18'' x 12''. Sprinkle with salt, lemon pepper or black pepper, crushed tarragon and dot with butter. Bring up ends of foil and seal securely.
- Place on the middle grill over medium heat for 15 minutes.

Serves 4

Stuffed Acorn Squash

1 medium-sized acorn squash
1 cup chopped apple
2 tablespoons brown sugar
2 tablespoons melted butter
Nutmeg

- Cut the squash in half, lengthwise, and scoop out the seeds and membrane. In a small bowl, mix together the chopped apple, brown sugar and butter. Fill the centre of each squash half with this mixture.
- Smear the rest of the cut part of the squash with butter and sprinkle all over with a little nutmeg.
- Wrap in a heavy-duty foil or two layers of regular foil. Place on the middle grill; cut-side up, over medium heat for 20 to 30 minutes, or until fork-tender.

Serves 4

Foil-Wrapped Corn-on-the-Cob

- Remove husks and silk from corn cobs and soak in cold water for 10 minutes. Shake off excess water and wrap in foil, individually, twisting the ends.
- Place on the lower grill over medium heat for 15 minutes.

Corn-in-Husks

- Peel back part of the husk from each cob of corn, and remove the silk. Butter the kernels and close up again.
- Place on the lower grill over medium heat for 15 minutes.

We found this was the favoured method of roasting corn as the flavour was much better.

finishing touches

Finishing Touches

'Finishing Touches', those added extras that make the meal perfect. While the coffee is brewing, throw on the prepared dessert. It usually only takes a few minutes and tops off the meal nicely. If you are concerned about the size of your guests appetites and whether you will have enough food, add a Bread to your menu. It makes an excellent filler. Be sure to try a barbecued breakfast. Great when you have overnight guests.

Mozzarella Bread

- Slice a loaf of French bread in 1-inch thick slices, not completely through the bottom crust so you create a hinge. Butter each slice generously. Place a ¼-inch slice of Mozzarella cheese in between each bread slice. Sprinkle a bit of crushed oregano on each slice of cheese.
- Place on a large sheet of aluminium foil and wrap up, securing tightly and pulling the loaf together.
- Place on the middle grill over medium heat for about 15 minutes, or until the cheese melts.

Garlic Bread

- Slice a loaf of French bread in the same manner as for Mozzarella Bread. Butter generously and sprinkle each slice lightly with garlic salt and chopped parsley. You may also use prepared Garlic Butter.
- Wrap securely in a large sheet of aluminium foil. Place on the upper rack over medium heat for 5 minutes, or until heated through.

Heating Rolls or buns

- You may thread the rolls onto a long metal skewer and brush the tops with melted butter, or just simply place the rolls on the upper rack over low heat for about 5 minutes.

Butters

- Cream the butter until soft and light. A food processor works well. Beat in the remaining ingredients. You may then turn into a small serving bowl **or** turn onto a sheet of waxed paper and shape into a cylinder. Wrap, chill and then slice into individual serving pats.

Garlic Butter

½ cup butter, softened
1 garlic clove, minced
or ½ teaspoon garlic powder
2 tablespoons parsley

Herbed Butter

½ cup butter, softened
½ teaspoon salt
Dash of pepper
1 tablespoon chopped parsley
1 tablespoon chopped chives
½ teaspoon crushed tarragon, and/or
½ teaspoon chervil

Lemon Butter

½ cup butter, softened
1 tablespoon lemon juice
½ teaspoon salt
Dash of pepper
2 tablespoons chopped parsley

Dill Butter

½ cup butter, softened
1 tablespoon lemon juice
1 teaspoon minced scallions
1 teaspoon dried dill weed
½ teaspoon salt
Dash of pepper
Dash of cayenne

Mustard Butter

½ cup butter, softened
3 teaspoons prepared mustard
½ teaspoon salt
2 tablespoons chopped parsley
Few drops Worcestershire sauce
Dash of pepper

Curried Butter (For Seafood)

½ cup butter, softened
1 tablespoon lemon juice
½ teaspoon salt
Dash of pepper
Pinch of cayenne
½ teaspoon curry powder

Fruit Kabobs

Apples - unpeeled, cut in 1 ½-inch wedges
Peaches - unpeeled, cut in 4 wedges per peach
Bananas - very firm, cut in 2 inch pieces
Oranges - peeled, section or cut crosswise into ½-inch thick slices
Pineapple - cut into 1-inch chunks
Apricots - whole and tender
Maraschino cherries

Marinades:

1. **2 tablespoons honey**
   2 tablespoons lemon juice
   1 teaspooon cinnamon

2. **2 tablespoons orange juice**
   2 tablespoons honey
   ½ teaspoon cinnamon

3. **2 tablespoons melted butter**
   1 tablespoon creme de menthe

- Select firm fruits. Cut the softer fruits in larger pieces than slow cooking harder fruits. You may use 6 inch wooden skewers for individual servings or 18 inch metal skewers.
- For the marinades, heat them up a little so they will blend together better. Brush on frequently during the cooking process.
- Use a very hot fire and turn frequently for all kinds of kabobs. I suggest that you place them on the middle grill over high heat for 10 minutes.

Spiced Pears

1 pear half per person
Lemon juice
Sugar
Cinnamon
Nutmeg

- Slice each pear in half, lengthwise from the stem to the eye, and scoop out the core. Lay on individual sheets of aluminium foil. Sprinkle with lemon juice and sugar and a light dusting of cinnamon and nutmeg.
- Wrap foil securely around each pear and lay on the middle grill over medium heat for 5 minutes.
- Serve with a maraschino cherry in the middle for color. It is also very nice with whipped cream on top.

Stuffed Pears

4 pears
¼ cup sugar
¼ cup melted butter
¼ teaspoon ground ginger
¼ teaspooon cinnamon

- Cut the stems off the pears and core from the top end, making a hole approximately 1-inch in diameter. Be careful not to core all the way through to the bottom. In a small bowl, mix together the sugar, butter, ginger and cinnamon. Stuff this into the pear cavities.
- Place each in the centre of individual pieces of aluminium foil, wrapping loosely and twisting at the top to seal. Place on the middle grill over medium heat for 5 minutes, until tender.

Serves 4

Baked Oranges

4 oranges
4 teaspoons butter
4 teaspoons brown sugar
Raisins
4 Maraschino cherries

- Peel and remove the pith from the oranges. Separate into four sections, partway through, being careful not to separate completely. In the centre of each orange place 1 teaspoon butter, top with 1 teaspoon brown sugar and about 10 or 12 raisins. Place a maraschino cherry on top of all this. Lay each orange on a sheet of aluminium foil, 8'' x 12''. Bring the sides of the foil up, forcing the orange together, and twist the foil together at the top to seal.
- Place on the lower grill over medium heat for 10 minutes.

Serves 4

Almond Peaches

1 peach per person
Almond extract
Cinnamon
Sugar
Maraschino cherries

- Slice each peach in half and remove the pit. Sprinkle one half with almond extract, cinnamon and sugar. Place a maraschino cherry in the cavity left by the pit. Top with the other half of the peach and wrap individually in foil.
- Place on the middle grill over medium heat for 7 to 10 minutes.

Baked Whole Pineapple

1 whole pineapple, with leaves intact
20 whole cloves
½ cup maple syrup
1 teaspoon ground cinnamon
Ice cream
Maraschino cherries

- Completely pare the outside off the pineapple, leaving the leaves intact. Remove the eyes and insert whole cloves in the holes. Remove a few spikes from the centre of the leaves and insert the pineapple on the spit. You may have to use a skewer to make the hole first. Secure with holding forks and wrap the leaves in foil. Place on the rotisserie and rotate over medium heat for 30 to 40 minutes, until tender, with the lid partway up.
- Baste frequently with a mixture of the maple syrup and cinnamon.
- When cooking time is completed, remove the pineapple from the spit. Slice it lengthwise down the middle and lay open on a platter. Cut into half-inch slices.
- To serve, place two pineapple slices on each person's plate with a scoop of ice cream in the middle and a maraschino cherry on top.

Serves 6

Stuffed Apples

4 large apples
4 teaspoons brown sugar
1 teaspoon cinnamon
1 teaspoon nutmeg
Raisins
4 teaspoons butter

- Core the apples from the stem end down, being careful not to go all the way through the bottom.
- In each centre, place 1 teaspoon brown sugar, ¼ teaspoon cinnamon, ¼ teaspoon nutmeg, approximately 10 raisins and 1 teaspoon butter. Wrap individually in aluminium foil, twisting at the top to seal.
- Place on the middle grill over medium heat for 10 minutes, until tender.

Serves 4

Nutty Apples

4 large apples
2 tablespoons melted butter
1 tablespoon brown sugar
1 teaspoon cinnamon
1 tablespoon flour
¼ cup chopped walnuts

- Core, peel and slice the apples. Mix all ingredients together in a bowl. Spoon out onto a large sheet of aluminium foil and bring up sides to seal securely.
- Place on the middle grill over medium heat for 10 minutes, until apples are tender.

Serves 4

Bananas-On-A-Spit

4 bananas
Corn syrup
Chopped walnuts

- Peel the bananas and cut each in half across the middle. Thread each half on a 6 inch wooden skewer. Roll each in a plate of corn syrup, then a plate of chopped walnuts. Transfer to a small piece of aluminium foil and roll up, twisting the ends.
- Place on the lower grill over low heat, turning a couple of times, for 5 minutes.

Children love these!

Serves 4

Marshmallow Surprize

Marshmallows
Candy

- Smarties or M & M's
- Chocolate-coated raisins
- Licorice pieces
- Small gumdrops

- Thread marshmallows on 18 inch long metal skewers. Toast over hot coals, turning constantly, until soft and lightly golden. Remove from the skewer and immediately insert a candy into the hole. Serve immediately.

Popcorn

- Lay out a strip of heavy-duty aluminium foil, 18'' x 12''. Pour onto the centre, 2 tablespoons vegetable oil and 2 tablespoons popping corn. Bring up ends of foil, leaving a large air space, and twisting at top to seal and make a pouch.
- Preheat grill to high heat. Holding the top of the pouch with tongs, shake 4 inches over the coals for a few minutes, until the popping stops.
- Open the pouch and pour melted butter over the popcorn and sprinkle with salt.

Serves 2

Breakfast Ideas

Bacon

- Place the griddle on the middle grill and preheat to medium. Spread the bacon slices out on the griddle. Continue cooking and turning until they are crispy.

A cast iron frypan will work as well but it doesn't have a grease catch around the perimeter as a griddle does.

Sausages

Some sausages can be cooked on the grill over the open flame. This will depend on the quality of the sausage as it can lead to the casings sticking to the grill and, consequently, rupturing the sausage.

I recommend using a barbecue griddle which will ensure even distribution of heat with no 'flare-ups' and result in a gold brown finished product.

- Place the griddle on the lower grill and preheat to medium-low. Oil the griddle lightly. Cook the sausages for 20 to 30 minutes, turning frequently.

Fried Eggs

Make sure your barbecue is level so that the eggs won't run into each other.

- Grease the griddle and place on the lower grill. Preheat on medium-low for 5-10 minutes.
- Crack the eggs onto the griddle and sprinkle with salt and pepper. Add a little grated Parmesan cheese if you like. Close the lid and cook for 5-7 minutes or until eggs are cooked the way you like them. They should be watched constantly so they won't be over-done.

Omelettes

When cooking omelettes on a griddle, you may find that when you pour the egg mixture onto the griddle, it tends to flow out of control. To prevent this from happening, make sure your griddle is preheated sufficiently so that the eggs will cook immediately and bond to the griddle surface.

- Place the greased griddle on the middle grill and preheat on medium-low for 5-10 minutes.
- Pour the egg mixture on the griddle and cook for 4 or 5 minutes. Turn gently and cook for an additional 2 or 3 minutes on the other side.

Pancakes

- Grease griddle with vegetable oil. Place on the middle grill and preheat for 5-10 minutes on medium.
- Pour the pancake batter onto the griddle and cook for 3 or 4 minutes on each side, with the lid down, until golden.

If you like, you may heat up a topping for the pancakes. Blueberry or cherry sauce or homemade jam are excellent. Pour into a small saucepan and place on the upper rack of the barbecue while preheating and cooking the pancakes. Serve on the side to pour over the pancakes.

Your Own Recipes

Your Own Recipes

Your Own Recipes

Your Own Recipes

Your Own Recipes

Your Own Recipes

Your Own Recipes

Your Own Recipes

Your Own Recipes

Your Own Recipes

Your Own Recipes

Your Own Recipes

Your Own Recipes

Your Own Recipes

Your Own Recipes

Your Own Recipes

Index